THE SHETLAND PONY

By Sara Green

Consultant:
Dr. Emily Leuthner
DVM, MS, DACVIM
Country View Veterinary Service
Oregon, Wisc.

BELLWETHER MEDIA • MINNEAPOLIS, MN

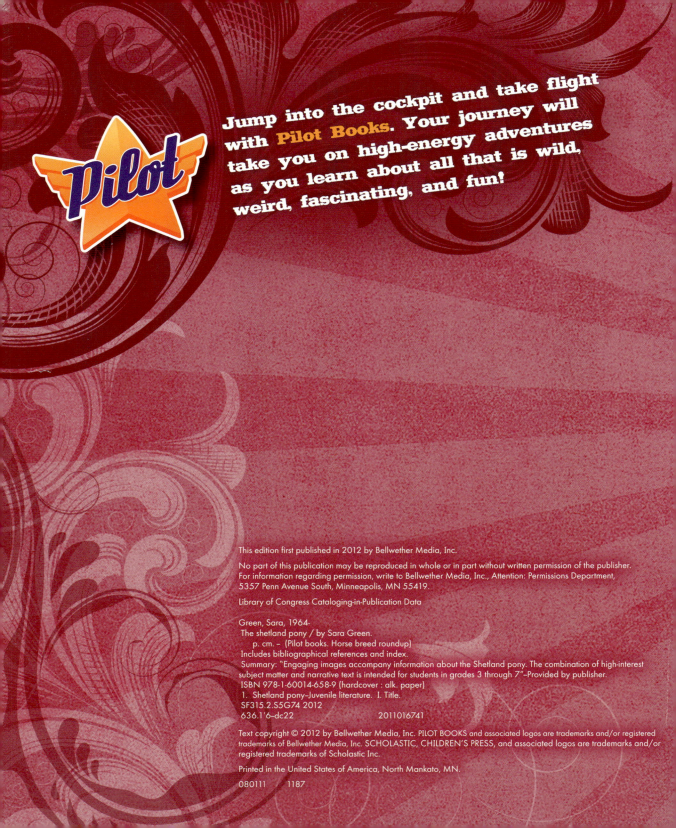

Jump into the cockpit and take flight with **Pilot Books**. Your journey will take you on high-energy adventures as you learn about all that is wild, weird, fascinating, and fun!

This edition first published in 2012 by Bellwether Media, Inc.

No part of this publication may be reproduced in whole or in part without written permission of the publisher. For information regarding permission, write to Bellwether Media, Inc., Attention: Permissions Department, 5357 Penn Avenue South, Minneapolis, MN 55419.

Library of Congress Cataloging-in-Publication Data

Green, Sara, 1964-
The shetland pony / by Sara Green.
   p. cm. – (Pilot books. Horse breed roundup)
 Includes bibliographical references and index.
 Summary: "Engaging images accompany information about the Shetland pony. The combination of high-interest subject matter and narrative text is intended for students in grades 3 through 7"–Provided by publisher.
 ISBN 978-1-60014-658-9 (hardcover : alk. paper)
 1. Shetland pony–Juvenile literature. I. Title.
 SF315.2.S5G74 2012
 636.1'6–dc22   2011016741

Printed in the United States of America, North Mankato, MN.

080111   1187

CONTENTS

The Shetland Pony.......4

Small Pony,
Long Journey............8

Harness Races,
Gymkhana, and
Miniatures............14

Glossary.............22

To Learn More..........23

Index................24

The Shetland Pony

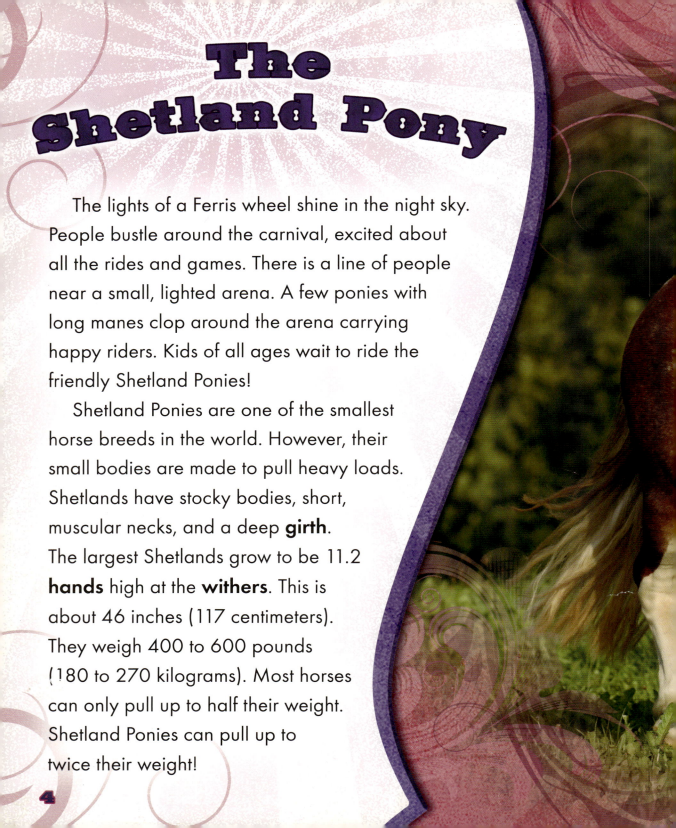

The lights of a Ferris wheel shine in the night sky. People bustle around the carnival, excited about all the rides and games. There is a line of people near a small, lighted arena. A few ponies with long manes clop around the arena carrying happy riders. Kids of all ages wait to ride the friendly Shetland Ponies!

Shetland Ponies are one of the smallest horse breeds in the world. However, their small bodies are made to pull heavy loads. Shetlands have stocky bodies, short, muscular necks, and a deep **girth**. The largest Shetlands grow to be 11.2 **hands** high at the **withers**. This is about 46 inches (117 centimeters). They weigh 400 to 600 pounds (180 to 270 kilograms). Most horses can only pull up to half their weight. Shetland Ponies can pull up to twice their weight!

Not Your Typical Horse

Although ponies are horses, they differ in many ways. Ponies usually have thicker manes, tails, and coats. They also have shorter legs, necks, and heads. They are often calmer, but more sassy, than larger horse breeds.

Shetlands have small heads with large, wide-set eyes and short ears. Many have a **dished face**. Their **muzzles** are small, but their nostrils are large. Strong hooves help Shetlands walk on rough ground.

Shetland coats come in a variety of colors and patterns. The most common colors are black and dark brown. Other colors include bay, gray, chestnut, and roan. Bay Shetlands have reddish brown coats with black manes and tails. Ponies with chestnut coats are the color of copper. Roan Shetlands have bay, black, or chestnut coats mixed with white hair. Some Shetlands have patterns like skewbald or silver dapple. Shetlands with the skewbald pattern have white patches on dark coats. Silver dapple Shetlands have very white manes that look silver. Their bodies are dark with flecks of white that give the coat a shimmer.

A Coat for Every Season

The Shetland's thick coat, long mane, and full tail keep it warm and dry in cold and rainy weather. In warmer seasons, the Shetland sheds the outer layer of its coat. The mane and tail, however, stay long and full.

Shetland Coat Patterns

skewbald

silver dapple

Small Pony, Long Journey

Shetland Ponies come from the Shetland Islands, located 130 miles (209 kilometers) north of Scotland. These islands have a harsh, cold climate and few plants. Shetland Ponies have lived on the islands for at least 2,000 years. They survived in this climate because their thick coats, long manes, and full tails kept them warm. They ate grass and the seaweed that washed ashore.

In the 1600s, Shetland islanders began to **domesticate** the ponies. They used the **hardy** Shetlands to plow their fields. They also used Shetlands to haul carts loaded with **peat**, seaweed, and supplies. The islanders used peat as fuel to heat their homes. They used seaweed as **fertilizer** for their crops. The hills of the islands were rocky and steep, but the sure-footed Shetlands could handle the terrain.

In 1842, a law was passed in Great Britain that changed the lives of Shetlands. The law said children could no longer work in mines. Shetlands began doing the work instead and became known as "pit ponies." They could fit into small spaces and pull heavy wagons loaded with coal. Thousands of Shetlands were sent to Great Britain to work as pit ponies. The number of Shetlands on the Shetland Islands had dropped from 10,000 to 5,000 by the late 1800s.

The life of a pit pony was not easy. Shetlands started working in the mines at the age of four. They spent nearly their entire lives underground. They were only allowed to go outside for short periods of time. However, most of the miners cared deeply for the ponies. They developed strong bonds with the Shetlands.

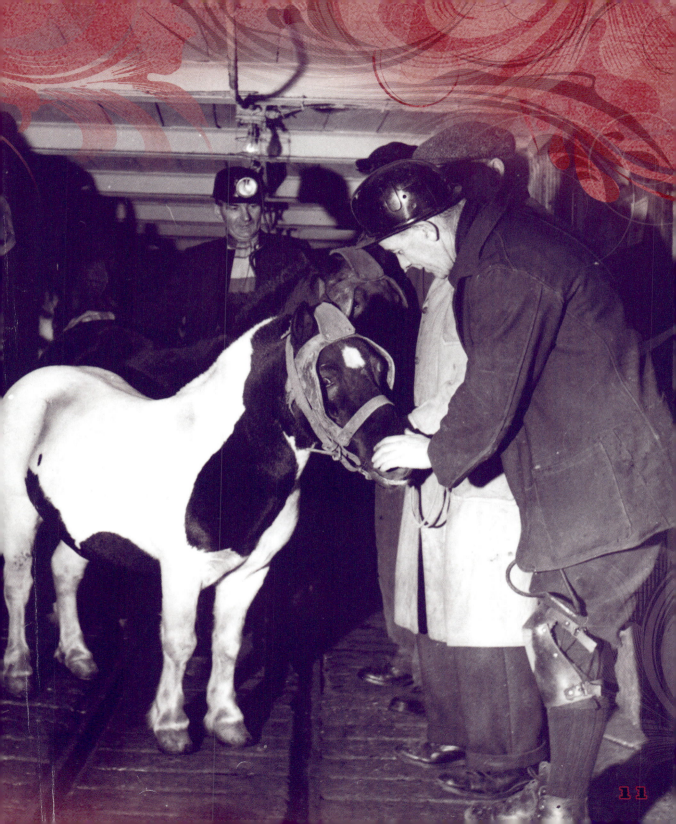

11

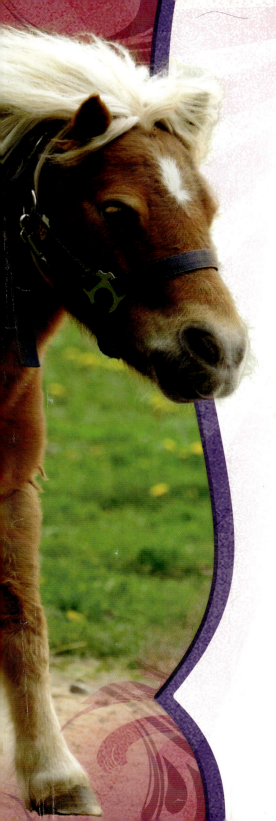

In the 1880s, people brought Shetlands to the United States for the first time. Some Shetland breeders wanted their ponies to have a more graceful look. Over time, they bred taller, slimmer Shetlands. These beautiful ponies became known as American Shetland Ponies. American Shetlands have longer legs and necks than their Scottish **ancestors**. Their bodies are thinner and less muscular. Most Shetland Ponies that live in the U.S. today are American Shetlands.

There are four types of American Shetlands. Each type has a slightly different look and **temperament**. The Classic American Shetland is tall, slender, and very gentle. The Modern American Shetland is an energetic pony that likes to perform. The short, shaggy Foundation American Shetland looks most like the Scottish Shetland. The Modern Pleasure American Shetland is friendly, quiet, and athletic.

Harness Races, Gymkhana, and Miniatures

Today, people use Shetlands for many different activities and sports. One of the most popular events is **harness racing**. Shetlands pull riders sitting in two-wheeled carts called sulkies. The ponies are attached to the sulkies by a harness and rope. The first pony to cross the finish line wins the race!

Gymkhana is another fun activity for Shetlands. Ponies and their riders compete in several timed events. Teams must work well together to succeed. One of the most popular gymkhana events is **barrel racing**. In this event, teams run as fast as they can around a course of three barrels. **Pole bending** is another favorite event. Ponies weave in and out of a line of poles without touching them.

Extra Small
The shortest Miniature Shetlands stand only 6 hands tall. That's just 24 inches (61 centimeters)!

The smallest Shetlands are Miniature Shetlands. People love the adorable look of these tiny ponies. Miniature Shetlands are gentle around children and make great **companion animals**. However, owning a Miniature Shetland is still a big responsibility. They require the same amount of care as full-sized horses.

Miniature Shetlands can do important work. Some of the most intelligent Miniature Shetlands become guide ponies for people who are blind. These highly trained ponies wear special harnesses. People hold onto the harnesses when they walk. The ponies help them cross streets safely and alert them to obstacles in their path. Guide ponies accompany their owners wherever they go.

Famous Shetland Ponies

Jack 16

Jack 16 was a stallion that lived in the mid-1800s. He belonged to Lord Londonderry, a wealthy mine owner. In 1870, Lord Londonderry set up a breeding farm on the Shetland Islands to breed more pit ponies. Jack 16 was one of his main breeding stallions. He fathered 49 foals. Many of today's Shetlands are related to Jack 16.

Algonquin

Algonquin was a Miniature Shetland that lived at the White House in the early 1900s. He belonged to Quentin, U.S. President Teddy Roosevelt's youngest son. Quentin once took Algonquin upstairs in the White House elevator. He wanted to cheer up his brother, Archie, who was sick in bed. Algonquin was so interested in his own reflection in the elevator's mirror that he didn't want to get out!

Curtiss-Frisco Pete

Curtiss-Frisco Pete, also called Frisco Pete, was a black American Shetland Pony born in 1950. Frisco Pete was supposed to pull wagons for a candy company. However, he proved to be too energetic for this job. In 1954, Frisco Pete began competing in horse shows. He went on to win most of the shows he entered. He was a six-time National Champion and was known as "King of the Shetlands."

The look and temperament of Shetland Ponies have made them popular around the world. Shetlands became strong and hardy living on the Shetland Islands. Today, they do not have to endure harsh living conditions. Both the stocky Scottish Shetlands and the slimmer American Shetlands live, work, and play around people. You might know Shetlands best as children's ponies. Their small size and friendly nature help children learn how to brush, feed, and ride horses. Children feel safe and comfortable around these ponies.

The tough, talented Shetland can do just about everything a full-sized horse can do. They participate in horse shows, races, and trail rides. Though Shetland Ponies are small in size, they're strong animals that make a big impression on people of all ages!

Glossary

ancestors—family members who lived long ago

barrel racing—a timed event in which riders race their horses around three barrels as fast as they can

companion animals—animals that provide friendship to people

dished face—a face with an inward slope between the eyes

domesticate—to tame; domesticated animals are used to living near people.

fertilizer—a substance added to soil that helps plants grow

girth—the distance around the belly of an animal

gymkhana—horse events that involve speed pattern racing; barrel racing and pole bending are gymkhana events.

hands—the units used to measure the height of a horse; one hand is equal to 4 inches (10.2 centimeters).

hardy—having the physical strength to endure harsh conditions

harness racing—an event in which a horse pulls a cart and rider; a harness attaches the cart to the horse.

muzzles—the mouths and noses of some animals

peat—rotting, water-soaked plants that build up over time; dried peat is used as fuel.

pole bending—a timed event in which riders weave their horses in and out of a line of poles as fast as they can

temperament—personality or nature; the Shetland Pony has a friendly, energetic temperament.

withers—the ridge between the shoulder blades of a horse

At the Library

Parise-Peterson, Amanda. *The Shetland Pony*. Mankato, Minn.: Capstone Press, 2006.

Rumsch, BreAnn. *Shetland Ponies*. Edina, Minn.: ABDO Pub., 2011.

Wedekind, Annie. *Little Prince: The Story of a Shetland Pony*. New York, N.Y.: Feiwel and Friends, 2009.

On the Web

Learning more about Shetland Ponies is as easy as 1, 2, 3.

1. Go to www.factsurfer.com.

2. Enter "Shetland Ponies" into the search box.

3. Click the "Surf" button and you will see a list of related Web sites.

With factsurfer.com, finding more information is just a click away.

Index

Algonquin, 18

American Shetlands, 13, 18, 20

ancestors, 13, 18

barrel racing, 14

body, 4, 6, 13

coats, 6, 7, 8

companion animals, 17

Curtiss-Frisco Pete, 18

domestication, 9

Great Britain, 10

guide ponies, 17

gymkhana, 14, 15

harness racing, 14

history, 8, 9, 10, 13, 18, 20

Jack 16, 18

manes, 4, 6, 8

mines, 10, 18

Miniature Shetlands, 16, 17, 18

pit ponies, 10

pole bending, 14

Scotland, 8

Shetland Islands, 8, 9, 10, 18, 20

size, 4, 16, 17, 20

tails, 6, 8

temperament, 13, 17, 20

United States, 13

work, 4, 9, 10, 17, 18

The images in this book are reproduced through the courtesy of: F1online / Age Fotostock, front cover, pp. 12-13; Tierfotoagentur / Alamy, pp. 4-5; Stoelwinder Stoelwinder / Photolibrary, p. 7 (top); Ellwood Eppard, p. 7 (left); Juniors Bildarchiv / Photolibrary, p. 7 (right); Jeremy Pardoe / Alamy, p. 8; General Photographic Agency / Getty Images, p. 9; Getty Images, pp. 10-11; Alun Jenkins / Alamy, pp. 14-15; Corbis / Photolibrary, pp. 16-17; Grebler M / Photolibrary, pp. 18-19; Bettina Salomon / Masterfile, pp. 20-21.